Gallery Books
Editor Peter Fallon
TIGHTROPE

Aidan Rooney

TIGHTROPE

Gallery Books

Tightrope
is first published
simultaneously in paperback
and in a clothbound edition
on 22 November 2007.

The Gallery Press
Loughcrew
Oldcastle
County Meath
Ireland

www.gallerypress.com

ISBN 978 1 85235 435 0 *paperback*
       978 1 85235 436 7 *clothbound*

A CIP catalogue record for this book
is available from the British Library.

Contents

No more à propos *preface is there than*
your heads going heavy hearing out my heart;

    and then my thinking: finally, now, I can
    send you both to bed and play the part

        of staying, praying, saying all a man
        can hope for for you both and for us all. A start.

for Cathal and Ciarán

PART ONE

*Things, in one's absence, gain
permanence.*
— Joseph Brodsky
'Café Trieste: San Francisco'

Aïsha's Charm

Into a bowl of water soothed
with three stigmas of saffron

and a yellow rose fished pre-dawn
from the still, reflecting pool

where she, come home and clean last evening,
had tossed her withered, red bouquet,

he dips his fingertips and tongue,
and begins to feel and love again.

The Stain

I might have gone in just to see
the megapixel make-up of
some shading round your eyes and mouth
evocative of a brightness that
it would be nice to bring back.

I promise though I've touched up just
a stain on the hand-me-down wedding gown
the healing tool made light work of.
So much more I could have done
and no one would ever know a thing.

Swimming at Barley Cove

Leaving the grown-ups to reapply sun lotion
on the little pitch of strand between two headlands,
when the only cloud around trawls off the ocean
a more than momentary darkening of the sands
you've left prints on, and wading out past hyper children
mollycoddled in wetsuits to body-surf the crests
of waves that drop them safely back, and swimming then,
beyond the warm undertow, where buoyance broadcasts
your exercise of freedom,
                                    your toes discover
awareness first, your feet so long kept on the ground,
and then your loins constrict to check all life before
you overhear the heart, above the whistle, pound
the newfound blood in ways that make no nonsense
of these near-life, out-of-mind moments, the far-flung
sun back out of the blue to overhaul what chance
you have, and nobody near to hear you sing your song.

The Book Her

1

On a tumble of stones beneath an O
in the wall around the Mental orchard
Rosie fishmouths out a wobbly halo,
lassoing me to accept the Silk Cut
she cups professionally forward
to my lips. A gun goes off. The racket
of inner overgrowth is beyond us:
dizzing flies in shot shrubbery, a slug
worming in every windfall's suppurant bruise.
We lie low in the wreckage of rock and rings
scarved around us, the faintly crackling drug
inhaled, puffed sunward, making light of things,
how the book her and the real me got mixed up.

2

Would you, she laughs, when I give her the gist
of last night, jooked beside her, take a drop
with me perhaps? Her mouth makes a light twist
round a gorgeous strawberry popped in whole,
its hot flesh melting, about as sassy
as they come. Harry looms behind her, rolls
his one straight eye, turns back to his Massey
and pulls her throttle for the ride back in,
patients drifting back with half-full buckets
to climb up on the trailer. Is it acting
the Oynie you are? I hear him nosey
through the slid window behind his bucket
seat where Rosie reads *Cider with Rosie*.

Survival

Scant caveat for the double hairpin turn
our 2CV failed to quite negotiate,

that sigmoid a hundred yards back, squiggled
on an amber triangle behind a tree,

would echo the roadkill we ended up beside,
over-easy, driver's side, a few miles

the far side of Falcarragh, were it not so far
along in its excited decomposition,

less the *bourdonnement* of bluebottles
than the cooperative wriggle of maggots

making heat in the bloated carcass someone'd
flung into long grass, roiling like a motor

at the heart of the badger, our own still ticking
over, one wheel spinning in mid-air, till

we tip it back on all fours and carry on,
the top rolled back, to the *Ostán* in Gweedore

for a swim and sweat, our pelts carving water
above our trawled shadows, then glistening side

by side on cedar bunks, aglow and pulsing
in the kind of heat that would make your breathing

something to think about if we hadn't talked,
then touched, putting all account behind us.

The Teapot Rockery

She must have taken the notion, some summer afternoon,
taking her tea and Marietta on the rug on the lawn out front,

of filling with clay to plant with pansies a pot never poured
right, not fit for company, and setting it out among the rocks

in a spot between two heathers we'd taken home from Bragan
when out for a run to the Mass Rock, and seen that it was good.

The Very Picture of Want

Waking, a woman who had planned on a boiled egg for tea
    after the Angelus
sees the bluish streak of bus go by to Armagh, Portadown,
    Belfast in the glass

of the only picture, and then the usual lozenge of shine the
    kitchen window casts
across a wound the smiling, long-haired man parts, the
    uncorrected clock, fast

she forgets now how long, melting too in the hot sweep and
    still rock of evening
a little cross burns through, its orange glow in the red dome
    for now unstriking.

Night will come on, into the picture, its cool stealth darkening
    names of children,
listed first to last in faded shades of biro a teacher neatly
    entered on the one line

left for them to come into the world to strike in time that
    same order of departure,
the cross picking up its pulse when all that was flickers and
    yields to the rapture

low-watt lumens make flesh, their hair let down, eyes locked
    in a sorrowful gaze,
the very picture of want, not much, a face to watch that stays
    the same and stays.

May Altar

in memory of Clare Rooney (1928-2000)

I THE VISIT

> *e la domanda che tu lasci è anch'essa*
> *un gesto tuo, all 'ombra delle croci.*
> — Montale

Last night you were living with the neighbours.
They showed up with their boys as they always do,
on the porch some weekend evening, bearing a salad,
a bottle of red, a six-pack for themselves, and you

fell right in after them, no introductions, wearing
one of your flowered summer skirts and carrying
the big cream, ceramic bowl you started bread in.
Everyone smiled and kissed hello and acted normal

except for you, a certain coolness in your manner
as if to show some hurt that you hadn't been invited.
The seared tuna came out perfect on the new grill.
The kids behaved. I expected you to scold us

for the fuss, no call for half of it, the new kitchen
you escaped to while we sat down to food. 'There's
a pretty little girl from Omagh in the county of Tyrone',
I overheard you sing, and when you left with them

you left with me a wheaten loaf with the deep cross
you liked to score on top, your white fingers disappearing
to tell beads in your apron pocket, your lips going through
the little motions of well-meant, recurring prayers,

the core of the bread, underneath, burning my palm.

2 LOST

A wind was in the room when the man woke
knowing he would never know how to die.
There was nowhere really left to hide but back
at being a boy in some secluded sun-warmed spot,
a place to spread the rug, lie down, a flat patch
in an unmown field, a dune in a summer seaside place,
repose he hoped his mother's eyes had found,
in extremis, before they had to seal them shut
on truths she must have come to know, so long
in silence and alone. 'Stop going through the rooms,'
he cried, 'and lie down dead.' But still she walked,
puzzled in familiar places, looking for children,
sensible shoes, a coat to go out in and get them,
wearing on her face the furthest thing from peace.

3 MAY ALTAR

Because you'd be disappointed
that Our Lady got no mention
in the various speculations
about your final, disjointed
movements, let me soothe that tension

and have in a vase appointed
budding lilies from your garden
to open for your assumption
in a place you'll find anointed
with blue, perpetual blossom.

4 NIGHT SCENT

Not wide enough to pass the mower through,
a crevice in the ledge seemed ideal
for raising herbs. Crawling with weeds, a yew
that hadn't thrived, we exhumed all the soil

and filled the spot with a loamy, black manure,
glistening promise as it fell from the slit
in the plastic. Last night a woman lay there,
crushing profusions of lavender and mint.

Since she looked like no one I knew I breathed
relief. A cool fragrance of pot-pourri
slipped in through the window's gauze, bequeathed
to pause in the bedroom dark, to bring you back to me.

5 THE SHOES

In the sightings she's seen as always going:
Mick, the Monday morning, to Mass in St Joseph's;
John, who'd give her a lift in the rain, the same
that chilly Tuesday. 'She was awful fit,'
he says, 'All go. And sure she'd lay into you
if you stopped at all.' Tuesday evening,
shortly after six, a man from Tyholland
saw her going in the road. 'You could tell
she wasn't right,' he reported. She must
have turned to try and make it back to home
where she wouldn't be seen in such a state,
the coat that wasn't on all the way dropped
on the sitting-room floor beside the shoes
she must have slipped out of and laid aside.

6 UNFINISHED NEFERTITI

Dynasty 18, reign of Akhenaten, 1353-1336BC, Quartzite,
Egyptian Museum, Cairo, JE 45547, most likely the work of
the royal sculptor, Thutmose

A clasp might fashion hair clamps shut your head. 'Extracted
for further tests,' the coronor whispers, as I finger and let fall

new-washed curls I haven't felt in years. An amethyst bruise
the side you lay on is turning white. And your mouth is off.

It wears a puss, a kind of collapse I want to set right. Every-
        thing
is wrong. Nothing overstated. Outside the heavy double
        doors,

the attendant with the key cups his smoke against the drizzle.
Next door, like Thutmose in his workshop, the undertaker
        fires

faience for the famous other bust of you — Miss Omagh,
        1948 —
while I wait in the county morgue with your exquisite head,

vacated and tenoned for hat or crown, my short vigil over
your polished face, prepared for inlays of glass, not enough

to find and bring you back to beauty, or send you forth
        complete.

7 STATUE

I will take and leave it. The house is as good
as empty. Less, too, she'd want to come with me
than stand here in the rain, watch over you who'd
want to *pray for us who have recourse to thee.*

Chansonette

In Oppidum
I live, a bum,
hair and clothes in tatters,

my home a tomb,
you might assume
I'm weary of chit-chatters.

But I'm post that
New Age, old hat,
that addles idler squatters;

with opium
to help me strum
this song the Mistral scatters,

I ask what sum
the tedium
mulling lofty matters?

Oppède-le-Vieux, July 2000

Montgomery

Was the one repeat in our school that year.
Kept to himself. Came and went. Said nothing.
What are they like? I asked once, shifting gear
in the dip of Bessmount Hollow to bring
myself alongside him the last stretch
to his house, all uphill beneath great trees
jackdaws made a racket in. Pretty much
like yours, he said, though shifting them's a breeze.

We hit a disco outside Aughnacloy.
And who might yous be when yous are at home?
these ones asked, their skirts awful summery
for the night that was in it. They had the foam
moustache of fresh pints licked off our lips, boy
's a boys, before we could say Montgomery.

Rosary

I wanted to join in with a decade
of Hail Marys one of your sisters had
started up. The easy, professional way
she slipped her beads out and lightly pressed
each one in turn between thumb and index,
moving right along, no nonsense, each one
that bit more melodious than the last.
You had yours out too, holding on to them
for dear life, your apron ones, the ones
we might say now you multi-tasked in.
I see you stir the roiling claret soup
a saucepan of currants we'd picked that morning
becomes, lacquering the wooden spoon
I'd wait to lick, and all the while your lips
impart a prayer.
                    But I thought I might
slip up, forget a line, or lose all count
the way father sometimes would. He'd double-
check with us, elbows on stools and zoning
out about the kitchen. None the wiser,
we'd end up saying a prayer too many,
and sometimes even another decade
added to the Sorrowful Mysteries
we'd tune back into, fingering along
the beads we got from Knock and Lourdes
in hard, cushy boxes. Yours go forward
with you. His are down there too, unworried.
God only knows the stuff they're made of,
I hear you wonder together, taking turns
to untether the interlace of stones
from each other's intricate little bones.

Dismissal

in memory of James Rooney (1910-82)

Three miles from Emyvale, in the townland of X, the sun will
    not show up
to catch drips on a five-barred gate where bullocks congregate
    in muck.

A low, snocemed house in a drumlin's grip hides behind its
    unclipped hedge.
Briars camber along the lane where staggered puddles regain
    enough composure

to mirror a stricken sky. It will rain shortly. The settled
    stones will be rinsed clean,
and the mud spatters on the shiny car parked out front will
    be erased. There is money

scattered on the front seats and floor. An elderly man lies by
    the hedge, shades
of plum and indigo on his balding scalp and face where the
    crowbar hadn't

smashed through skin and bone to his last inkling of what
    has come to pass,
how the young man he picked up next the Hillgrove must
    have gotten it all wrong —

or right enough to sleep before he'd trump his story up,
    explain how long it took
to fend off attentions, how hard it was to stay the rage of an
    old man's affections.

Sleeping Valley Boy

after Arthur Rimbaud's 'Le Dormeur du Val'

A river sings through it, this spot of greenery
where crazy grass hangs out and hooks quicksilvers;
the sun, from its high and mighty scenery,
shines: the valley buzzes with its random slivers.

A boy soldier, mouth open, helmet off, blue
watercress pressing round the nape of his neck, catches
a little shut-eye, spreadeagled beneath the blue;
on his green-haloed face daylight rains down patches.

Feet up on wild iris, he sleeps smilingly the way
a sick child might. Just a little nap, you might say.
Mother Nature, he is cold; warm him in your temple.

No fragrance makes his nostril flutter, no flies are on
the hand-on-chest of this boy in the no-fly zone.
He sleeps in the sun. Two red holes spot his right temple.

Francis Bacon and the Hen

Men are alike in this:
whosoever gets
a good idea leaps,

as Bacon did (or
so the story goes)
out of the coach

to have a common hen
slain and gutted, raring
to stuff a ball of snow

into her cavity, ice
as good a cure
as salt, and truth

an insufficient end.
He knows exactly
what he's about,

a hand in the bird,
what way Highgate is,
the price advancement

pays, and for three
listless, snowbound days
he drifts in and out,

feeling the nip of death.

Recordings

So hungry, I think I broke my nose. *Is maith an t-anlann
an t-ocras.*
Is minic a bhris béal duine a shrón. Your mouth is one
yummy sauce.

Green is remotely beautiful, isn't it? *Ní fiuchann áilleacht
an pota.*
Is glas na cnoic i bhfad uainn. Stony black hills. A lot of
pot.

Mind that hot trout in your trousers. *Níl aon tinteán mar
do thinteán féin.*
Is fearr breac sa phota ná bradán sa bhfarraige. More like a
wild salmon.

Short married couple walkie-talkie. Queens of heart.
Giorraíonn beirt bóthar.
*Ón lá a bpósfaidh tú beidh do chroí i do bhéal agus do lámh
i do phóca.* So far.

The young give a lot of head. *Ag duine féin is fearr a fhios
cá luíonn an bhróg air.*
Bíonn ceann caol ar an óige. Old shoes pinch. I know. Get a
new pair.

Baa baa black sheep. Skin alive and hang 'em high. Fly.
Drochubh, drochéan.
*Ní túisce craiceann na seanchaorach ar an bhfraigh ná
craiceann na caorach óige.* Foregone.

Don't have a cow at Christmas! *Bíonn chuile dhuine lách go
dtéann bó ina gharraí.*
Nollaig bhreá a dhéanann reilig teann. Be nice! Or you'll
end up pushing up daisies.

Morning sex and the day's shot. A name for fondness. *Is túisce deoch ná scéal.*
An té a dtéann cáil na mochéirí amach dó ní miste dó codladh go méanlae. Tell-tale.

Ask the cat did she hide the bottle? *Ní ólann na mná leann ach imíonn sé lena linn.*
Dearmad bhean an tí ag an gcat. And the fiddle. Party on!

The grass wasn't good enough for him. *Bíonn súil le muir ach ní bhíonn súil le tír.*
Mair, a chapaill, agus gheobhaidh tú féar. Horse overboard! Have no fear.

Get your highness the puck out of here. *Ní dhéanfach an saol capall rás d'asal.*
Cuir síoda ar ghabhar agus is gabhar i gcónaí é. A fine ass on him. Can he hustle!

Hey cutie! Be my heart candy. *An bhean atá dóighiúil is furasta a cóiriú.*
An rud a líonas an tsúil líonann sé an croí. All I want is to put clothes on you.

No homes to go to. Can't get rid of them. *Mol an óige agus tiocfaidh sí.*
Bí go maith leis an ngarlach agus tiocfaidh sé amárach. Aren't you lovely!

If she thinks she can turn off the heat. *Is folamh, fuar teach gan bean.*
Is teann madra ar a thairseach féin. I'd set the dog on her if I had one.

Accident

The river brought out the wild in Quigley.
That once he got himself all go he forgot
to let go of an elder with the spring in it.
It was the biggest laugh, and he screamed too
when he found himself catapulted on
to a raft of rapids going down the North
in a serious high water. The flood
took weeks to climb down out of the fields,
invite cows back to investigate with drool
the blank slate sky in the Blackwater.
The summer drought came on. We learned to swim
in the slimy shallows, the river down
to its draped stones, and the cows witnessed
our forgetfulness. It was all kept quiet.

Indian Summer

after Charles d'Orléans' 'Rondeau de Printemps'

The weather has dropped its anorak
of widespread, scattered showers,
and taken to draping the country's bowers
with spangles of light and shellac.

Every bird and beast and hack
sings well within its powers
now the weather's dropped its anorak
of widespread, scattered showers.

River, spring and mountain creek,
in filigreed attire,
show off their silver-smithery;
everyone's going maniac.
The weather has dropped its anorak.

Mode

Le haut got up in a *boléro, corps* in a *bustier,*
basques tight in a *mini-jupe* from Jean Paul Gaultier,
she slipped into my *petit soir, défrichant des territoires vierges,*
through *mousseline noire* by Guy Laroche, she sensed I was
    on the verge
of a *crise* of sorts unless I'm tossed *les clefs de sa belle Clio,*
sièges haberdasheried *tout en cuir,* Solaar on the stereo,
as we sped to *un startup*-hosted *boum* in the so-so *seizième*
where, *alanguie joue*'d like Vanessa P karaoke-ing Eminem,
elle dit yo, 'sup, pack my heat, *tu me trouveras travaillée,*
mon cocktail infinitely *explosif,* pure *Brut de Fabergé.*
Under the tarp of her billowy *blouson* slit with *petits plis*
extravagance and classicism *me semblaient* pretty please
au rendez-vous, indémodable, bestowed on an uppity *meuf,*
replete with *suspens pneumatique, Citroën DS 19.*

We piled in — Papa, Nicole, the pair of us —
and fired up on Diam's all the way to *Quick,*
    where a gathering of next door's *danseuses*
    pigged out on what wasn't a '*Big Mac*
        at all, *mesdemoiselles,* but a *Big Cheese*',
    the young Paddy-whack
        working the *caisse*
        quite quick,
            his excuse
            le smic.

Like down out of *un OVNI* it was, a cushy *descendue*
into what the *abat-jour, trottoir* to-do has to do
with dawn whitening the basilica, the condiment man *d'antan*
on *rue Lepic* in the *va-et-vient* of wanton women
talking Toulouse-Lautrec, his black *basilic* bunched in lassoes,
rien de spécial going down but *bien-serrés* at *zincs,* Picasso
Wuz Here graffitied on the up of a step to *Place de Tertres,*
charclos adoze in a bit of a wood with bottles where, after

I had a Dolce, she a Gabbana, we got the boot to FNAC,
himming and hamming *à la queue leu leu*, a cerulean pack
of *Gauloises Blondes* between us, for *Astérix chez les Hibernais*,
and a right *moue, look Cowgirl Urbaine*, came over her. How
   you say?
'*My pool is lane? Woolpool? Viens nager dans mon luxe et mon
   baroque.*'
Was I cool with that? Was I ever! She was an island. I was a
   rock.

A dose of the scabies, had the *danseuses*,
or some such *fièvre aphteuse*, a *genre* of tick
     got under the skin to *mange, démange*, insinuate clothes
     and play such parasitical, itchy havoc,
          le show can-can was a no-can-do, a no-flooze
          coup de pipe à coc-
              a, petit, grand (you choose),
              a *clop*-burned hole and gum, the trick
                 to fit the lid with two straws,
                 fais gaffe for *flics*.

Ghizlaine. I finally got it out of her. *Cinq cents et conque*.
I might have been in the back of a *voiture banalisée*, conked
out from a close brush, *crâne rasé*, bomber-jacketed *façon
   Belstaff*
or, *vogue motard anglais*, fronting a Yamaha 500 round
   Belfast
in straights and eighteen holes, *rira bien qui rira le dernier*,
on te trouvera si tu récidives, had she been less yeah yeah,
had less yen to *danse*, it dawned on me. I had an *apéro*,
she an *aperçu*, of *noir avec des touches de rose pâle*, or so
it looked to me. *Camouflash Guerre de Golfe*. Either way,
   it had *Tati*
written all over it, *pret-à-porter, Barbès*. Her hair was natty

with a clip kind of comb in it going *nulle part*. I like party, she
  goes,
rien en dessous, and gave a little Brazilian *danse de la chaise*
up on the *péripherique*. I stepped out for the blues at the *sortie
Stade de France*. Too *pétillante* by far. Couldn't keep it over 40.

Extract

Forgiveness, begged from the shaky indigo of a gas fog,
back then the way to go, genuinely sorry I'd kicked her
half way through extraction when, like a boa constrictor,
she reared up on me, hissed, spat, then lit up a half-grass fag

right there in the county clinic, mother outside, no bother
to her, two molars left hanging in the cheek of me, a wee brat,
pleading in tongues that she finish off her joint, then me, *caveat
emptor*, say nothing, it'll be our little secret. I'd no other

choice but pass out — fast forward here — a clean hygienist
bent on my contentment, her children's impeccable dentition
smiling at the wall opposite where gobs, in stages of attrition,
bare their gingivitis. Thanks be, I shivered and, sighing, wished

to doze forever in that rocket chair, admire her steel spittoon
that swirled away my blood-flecked drool, the plastic cup
with its own little tap, the suction wand going apoplectic,
post-rinse, at fresh saliva, me wondering if she feels it too soon

for us to get serious. She questions from behind a half a bra
cupping her jaw, but even still I catch a lovely aroma of apple,
a hint of mint the giveaway she just flossed, aloe, maple,
and a miscellany of other mystery sugars. *A-ah a a-ah*, I baa,

to which she extracts her tools, holding them over my face
like she's taking a break from knitting, or wondering if I'm what
she ordered last time at Siam Palace, if I come with kumquat.
Abracadabra, I whisper, now I can, beseeching every grace

to grant I never come to, toothless, in that other scary place.

PART TWO

The art of losing isn't hard to master;
so many things seem filled with the intent
to be lost that their loss is no disaster.
                    — Elizabeth Bishop
                              'One Art'

Tightrope

Both how, when I pulled the front door
this morning to let the sun in,
some night class of spinner had strung
from one jamb to the other
the flimsiest funicular
that, now a waft of light and air
enters to liven the dusty house,
passes lightning bands of silver
along its barely visible floss
as if to make sure all is clear,
and why, is just beyond us, unless
some huge jump needed to be taken.

Orb Web

Turns out not one but two
genera of spider —

aeons ago, back in
the Cretaceous age —

embarked upon the same
inventive business —

in parallel, but separate,
with all three requisites

for success: work that is
hard, long and done alone —

of turning out a web
designed to capture prey —

the one with fibres spun
and hung with beads of glue,

the other cast in silk
the spider combs to Velcro —

both inimitably
in the circular house-

hold, iconic fashion
that, globally, caught on.

Salade Garnie

Drizzle the wall of a vast bowl
with virgin oils, olive and nut,
one acquiescent truffle drip,
a touch of lemon zest, then pitch in

loosed sheaves of baby greens, butter-
head lettuce, arugula, cress,
spinach and sorrel, purslane shoots
to cool the liver, and not much

bergamot, cilantro, basil,
a little lovage for its salt
oomph, delicate anise of myrrh,
dandelion, sweet marjoram;

toss and garnish with the blue tops
of wild hyssop, umbels of cream
archangelica, to soften skin
flaxen-petalled calendula,

nasturtium spurs whose pepper
nectar the hummingbird hums to,
primrose, borage, rosemary, sage
and vitamin-rich *viola*

odorata, mustard and pansies,
elderflower to neutralize,
yarrow to sedate the heart's great burn
that wants to make you such a salad.

Home Song

a tribute to Ray Charles

If only it was he *came home and found you gone*.
Torn up pretty bad, he'd have broken into song
all heart had left to say: *come back, and do me wrong*.

That holler from the gutter, don't it right the wrong?
Can pity ease the heartache so given to the song
his longing turns to mine alone, and off I'm gone

to Georgia, with his misery, mystic soul, gone
in the mind to what he owns, America's song
to heartbreak, 'America the Beautiful'. What's wrong

with love is pain. Too big a country can go wrong
in the head and like it. *She puts me down.* Her song
too late seduces *I'm a fool for you*. I'm gone

way cross town, to freedom's honky-tonk back home, gone
and done and gotten simply over how the next song
might have gone. A love song. It says: love does no wrong.

Insalata

Again a summer salad — assorted greens
we'll not this time bother to go into,
and whatever else the internally-
weeping fridge recommended, the lot

tossed with the usual balance of oils,
some citric, herbs from the garden,
then laid out on a platter and topped
with shavings of *parmigiano* — wilts.

The blades of the ceiling fan on slow
keep cool the knives they pass round
without so much as a hum, and the forks
do well to keep their four tines down.

A stick of butter languishes in its dish
and the cuts of bread we've always liked
sliced diagonally have taken on
that little crust they shouldn't ever have.

And yet this unremarkable young *Rhône*
has opened up agreeably to the nose.
Currant and chocolate notes — all that.
It holds its redness nicely next the glass.

And these *niçoises* bathed in sesame
could not slip more bitingly sweet
off their little stones onto the tongue.
I gather they'll talk once you come home.

Ode to Cassandra

after Pierre de Ronsard's 'Ode à Cassandre'

Hey, sugar! Let's check out the rose
that — wasn't it just this morning? — exposed
its crimson garment to the sun,
to see if she has kept intact the pressed
pleats of her crimson dress,
so totally like your complexion.

Alas! See how, now, in such brief space,
my sugar — and so decidedly, alas! —
she's let her good looks wilt and fall.
O nasty mother, Nature, that you are,
for giving such a lifespan to a flower
that she lasts just from sun-up to nightfall.

And so, my sugar, accept as truth,
right now while you still have your youth
at the peak of its unplucked bounty,
sow, mow, gather all you can reap:
as with this flower, old age will creep
and lay waste to your beauty.

Eel at Market

the closer
the monger's
hacksaw cleaver
came
to the head
held down

the wider
the conger's
fang-full yawn
became
a manner
of crown

The Woman who was Pushed into the Sea

Peace is a disposition for benevolence, confidence, justice.
— Baruch Spinoza

The woman was pushed into the sea
not — coos cool Miss Laughter (*Poultry Co-Op*
emcee), passing her blade across her knee —
because she grew chickens in her own coop;

nor was she pushed — as McAnaly's sister,
(town therapist and telepathist) felt
called on to add — because someone pushed her
or because she kept herself to herself;

that woman was pushed into the sea —
rose Mrs Prim (chair, *Horticultural
Society*) — not because her roses
rose licentiously out of control;

nor was she pushed — according to Ms Noop
(*WatchDog Unit*, two picket fences over)
because she once frightened the living poop
out of my dearly belovèd Rover;

I couldn't push — Ms Basket makes the case
as Chief of Operation *Homeland Sleuth* —
I held back because I support the cause
of community vigilance and truth.

As do I and I — leap up twins Raptor,
Miss Concepta and Miss Assumpta,
on behalf of the *Silver Ring Thing* chapter —
though we can conceive of no idea

why the woman was pushed into the sea.
I'd like to *ditto* — points out Miss True North
(*Boundaries of Land and Sea* head trustee) —
all everyone's already said, and set forth

that the woman was pushed into the sea
for no good reasons we here should prolong.
Clearly, she drifted south and saw the sea
unwind its ropes for those who don't belong.

Astronomer

*Last night I heard Emerson give a lecture . . . It was like a beam
of light moving in the undulatory waves, meeting with occasional
meteors in its path.*
— Maria Mitchell (1818-1889)

In the gesture of one who guides the blind
or a blind-folded, incumbent lover
she draws him up a steep and narrow stair
into a kind of lighthouse light. What glare
there is is all moon, the astronomer
in her adjusting down the wick to find

what, earlier, she had isolated:
a nebula in Cassiopeia;
a comet's steadfast disintegration;
stars of her self-circumnavigation.
He would like to say that the whole idea
of closing distance is overrated,

that the more one sees of the universe
the less one is capable of seeing.
But he's been so long away he humours
her instead. And then there've been the rumours
about the island. Long past believing
what she can't see she gives, chapter and verse,

proof of their integrity, his try-pots
burning through the night, in full 360
3-D, as all the pleasure boats can do
is twinkle little stars. She floats a few
past his opinion of the world, a trick she's
learning, to learn to read his inmost thoughts.

Among the Wrecks

I THE 'ST JOHN'

foundered October 7, 1849, off First Cliff, Scituate

From Boston, scores of Irish set out South.
An urchin peels off handbills headed *Death!*
And Daniel Ward, outside his first, new house,
grooms three young sons for the gruesome prospect.

The *Longfellow* will not pass at 10 o'clock.
The sea a seasonal nor'easter broke
subsides enough to gather round the rocks
the bodies of the lost and their effects.

The Ward brothers tend, up and down the beach,
to horses fastened to the shoreline fence.
Their father wades through wreckage to detach
ship fragments from the arms of emigrants.

A mother who'd come over in advance
parts the crowd around each rough deal box
laid on a grassy stretch above the beach.
In one she finds her sister's and her infant's

remains recovered from the seaweed
a farmer resumes drawing from the tide.
And three days pass before the mother died
and Daniel Ward again nailed down the lid.

2 'IRISH MOSS'

established circa 1850, Peggotty Beach, Scituate

On days like this — full moon, full sun — he'll haul
on both low tides. Heaped above the gunnels,
his dory rides the light, incoming swells
that set him down beside the barrow creel.

He forks the wet moss in, then heaves the barrow
along a path of planks to where a row
of yesterday's sun-dried, blackened draw
turns already purple. He wipes his brow

and overturns the load. The boys have taken
the best part of the day off work to work.
One rakes, another hauls, the third soaks
each band of moss with water from the firkin.

The bands, now spread again, assume those hues
that moss consistent with its spectrum goes.
Purple blanches to pastel shades of blue,
then lavender, then pinks, the last blush

the same light amber tint the sun-touched
sky, then ocean, pick up at dawn and dusk.
Out around Minot Light, the long light shakes
the length his rake goes down to tear at sunken rocks.

3 THE 'FOREST QUEEN'

foundered February 28, 1853, Second Cliff, Scituate

Even the ever-wheeling, scything gull
has taken refuge from the thick snowfall.
The sails of the barque *Forest Queen* are furled,
as should, from flying jib to gallant sail

in most seamanlike a manner. A lull
in the whiteout allows the crew and all
forty immigrants to leave the vessel
and put ashore until the storm dwindles.

Captain and crew are quartered at the Wards
where Charlotte Ward and the ship's steward
pass out a bisque to thaw the blood. Afterwards,
her best blancmange buoys spirits. The blizzard

redoubles. Main and mizzen topmast shorn,
for two days straight the barque lies broadside on.
The sea recoils, then rolls at her again.
And then she bilges, writhes truck to keelson,

her manifest strewn across the rock-strewn bed:
skins, gin (London Dry), pig iron, bags of seed,
indigo and — now she lists to starboard —
ballast ingots of, some say silver, some say lead.

4 THE 'BIG HOUSE'

erected 1854, First Cliff, Scituate

So, to return — in kind — kind services,
the same said lead Daniel Ward salvages.
And in consideration of finances
settled to grant all deeds, he mortgages

the wherewithal to build himself a house.
A big house. Eleven rooms. Two chimneys.
On ten fields, five salt marshes, cliff meadows
bounded southerly and easterly by sea.

On sills of oak attached to granite blocks
sunk ten feet deep in the cliff's bedrock
posts rise. Beams hewn from Vermont hemlock
are windlassed up to joist and purlin pockets.

The Eve of All Saints. Charlotte Ward watches,
from a high window hung six over six,
her children moving in their few effects.
Plans for a *Meeting House for Catothicks*

advance, but the town's mossers cannot wait.
To the *Big House*, by causeway and culvert,
they join, in droves, a big man come, to celebrate
the first Mass said to be said in Scituate.

5 THE 'RIALTO'

foundered March 20, 1861, Fourth Cliff, Scituate

All afternoon the petrel walked on water.
The shearwater that faced the wind to tear
away from breakers forsakes the shelter
a crevice in the cliff cannot assure.

The day's squalls morph, come night, to all-out gusts
that thrust the sprays of sky and sea against
each other and all else. Snow bursts encrust
with rime the *Rialto*'s rails and main rigging —

its ensign in ribbons, Union down —
where only the captain, barely clinging on,
is seen. The Lyle gun fires a good, tight line
to set the breeches buoy and pull him in.

A colossal swell erupts, lifts and crashes
the after-house among the savin bushes.
Moss syrup. Whiskey. A hard rub has his
blood on course again. He knows where he is

the day after, able to sit up across
from a cross on a wall of the *Big House*.
A drift the shape of a low wave wreathes the place
in white and peace. He's at a loss.

A loss to tell much of himself, to know his loss:
his ship with a hold of timbers to build a house
in scraps not long enough to build a box for each
of three young sons being borne up from the beach.

Call

When you say you miss the taste, touch, scent, sounds
I made in the making of love to you,
we best not see each other, do you
mean to say this is the way your head sounds
out your heart? If so, I'll get over you
the way you say you want. Let's not meet. Sounds
like a plan, even if it all resounds
in the heart as feeling wrong. I'll love you
anyway, somewhat for the heck of it,
but more because I do. I could have died
laughingly today, right before you called,
before I'd know more what to make of it,
when my son said he wished we could keep died
and just do away with killed. Then you called.

Shame

I would wake up early toward the end
and turn around. I wanted to pretend
that we could be still lovers in the bed.
And I would look so long that you'd look dead.

Croustade

He loves to watch her fingers
cut cuts of cold butter in,
the flour become crumb
she'll sprinkle ice-water over,
incorporate with spoon, form,
and turn out on the counter.

Then he will go about picking
soft, sun-bursting fruit: wild
blueberries he's a fool for,
raspberries, pectin-loaded logan-
and boysenberries, and not forget
the sweet Cherokee blackberry.

He loved to watch her leave
her edges ragged, rimming
the dough-conforming bowl,
then pile right in a mound
of his unadulterated berries,
no spice, no sweet, no citrus.

Then he would go about whipping
up a batch of cream to match
the unglazed crust now going golden,
the medley of juices beginning
to bubble round the edges, brim,
then burn on the oven bottom.

Men at Work

Have X and Y? my neighbour wants to ask,
aligning pointing fingers, then drawing them
apart in the adroit gesture of one
about to indicate a box but drawing
just the lid. We are taking a breather,

my neighbour from across the way and I,
from shovelling the snow snowploughs have banked
at the foot of our drives. *They have,* I have
to say, then joke, *Must be something in the snow
down the even-numbered side of the street.*

A plough rasps past trying to stay on top
of snow that shows no sign of letting up.
The streetlamp overhead comes on to stage
its silent night light-show around itself,
briefly starring flakes falling within reach.

It's not easy, he says, crossing over,
and getting stuck into the ridge the plough
has turned. We catch up on each other's work,
our kids, the latest outs on bikes and boats,
putting our backs back in to the clearing

of the snow. The cedars that sag around us
bear their share of it. A branchful plummets
with a thump, and the branch springs back relieved.
Abominable snowmen that we are,
we dig beneath its weight, then shake it off.

Around the Clock

*Material for this poem taken from Police/Fire log of Friday, June 4
— Saturday, June 5, 2004, Hingham, Massachusetts. True identities of
all officers and victims have been suppressed.*

Out front of *Brewed Awakenings*, Hingham,
Officer Quicksolver's car ticks over.
The night is young. He feels the medium,
hot regular from the next town over's

Dunkin Donuts constrict the scalp his barber
buzzed that morning. Midnight now. Not a wrinkle
agitates the plate glass of the harbour.
Pumps asleep, at *Texaco* and *Mobil*,

do not anticipate the first blush brush
of dawn the slip to the water covets. Along
the two intersecting streets, a flush
of fusion bistros expose decors songs

paused on iPods cannot cheer up. Ex-
tractor fans, on low, do not distinguish
the idle from intense, or G from X,
of chatter cut and vacuumed, extinguished

like cigarettes in salt, outside, sidewalkward.
At *Tosca* the oversized, unlovely
lady on the wall makes no comment awkward.
She croons her aria superlatively.

Then, 1:25 a.m., intercept.
Union St, flag burned, hanging upside down,
vulgar remarks on it. Must have slept,
thinks Quicksolver. Also, speeding up and down

the street, an MV on High. Another
on Free smacks a tree. After 4, Rhodes
Circle, a resident reports brother
stole his wallet. Quicksolver loads

up again, this time at *Krispy Kreme*. Female
wants to speak with him re. brother. Appeals
for backup and picks up a *tamale*
in Weymouth at the all-nite *Taco Bell*.

All agents engaged. Officer Blowholes
issues fines to early-bird clam diggers
scouring the tidal flats for little holes.
PO Eddie Pusiano, who figures

the light commute kicked in along 3A
is too ripe to neglect, nails a *Shamrock
Landscaping* pickup that failed to see the
STOP sign parked behind a tree. Damn bad luck

that. *Licence and registration?* — *Register
this*, the driver whispers, and drops him
with the door. The bumper sticker's math twister,
26 + 6 is 1 or something,

does not add up for PO Pusiano.
The driver floors it back across townlines.
Entering Hull, lights up a Marlboro.
At 8:29 a.m., Main, a 9-

11 reports allergic reaction.
Bee sting. Animal Control Officer
paged. Responds: tied-up; Crooked Meadow Lane,
dog struck; chipmunk under furnace; fox under

porch; Liberty Pole Rd, barking dog on deck.
9 a.m., Summer, theft: Blowholes, respond.
INS notified. Cleaner suspect.
Melville Walk, report of trespasser. Pond,

operator of black MV speaking
to young females. Ship, youths on scooters. Free
again, 10 a.m., landscaper peeking
through windows. 11 a.m., Attorney

Grace Wanting reports *Attorney at Law,*
Esq sign taken from property. Private
investigator advised. Suspected scofflaw.
Noon. Sunny. 80 degrees. A privet

hedge goes in on Pleasant. A painter paints.
A roofer fires his nail-gun on a roof.
The Hingham Town Hall clock, on high, acquaints
itself with getting stuck again. Aloof

bells at the Benedictines peal for calm.
A monk on High out walking cites a psalm
to help him meditate upon the Angelus.
Lincoln, water leak. Beach, breeze. Whiting, odour, gas.

Babble

You could say you were having none-of-it
in any of countless, Godforsaken,
good-as-dead fire-tongues — in Inuit,
en Provençao, as Gaeilge, not to mention
sign, smoke, a cut above the wrist, a smote
of love's telepathos, or 'tis a scratch
and sniff of kiss-ass English — but it's not
what you do but the way, sweet fuck, they watch,

then do you in, the cottony body
bag, the what you'll pick out of your kisser mouth
with broken fingers, present your lady,
you who makes me think in Mass when I could-
n't get you out of my head: if God is
love, my love, then who better when in Rome?
We lie, stroke luck. We make no din. Do me.
It's all good. Chill. This bed our centre is.

Spring Court

Two pigeons, making out, high on a bough
of a tree I am sorry to say is dead.
The girl one has chosen. The way he fanned
and dragged his tail, curtsied, sent shivers down
an especially iridescent neck,
strutted, then drove after her in circles,
has brought her here to teach him how to kiss.

He gets it right, how she likes it, and not
what might have made the self-delighting his.
Her bill thrust inside his, she nips the tongue,
exciting him to jump her bones, straddle
her up-pointed ass the short while it takes.
Arising then, the cock shakes out his wings,
claps twice, alights and makes to kiss again.

Proof

Turns out, alas, God sat down on the job.
Not very long, thank God, but long enough
to make the Earth not absolutely round.
So, like a ball someone sat upon, Earth

got thrown a bit off-kilter — oblately
spheroid — such that, were Zidane to snipe
a sure-fire, frozen rope on goal, Earth
would pull a serious Beckham and bend

God-knows-where, just another shooting star.
Earth, in fact, is quite flat: Everest's peak
is not even close to being the furthest point
from the hell-like, dead centre of the Earth.

This inconvenient bulge we've just found out
the Earth's plump middle wears reports, in parts,
a river flowing upward for a stretch,
slant stalactites, bats hanging upside up,

explains, in part, imbalances and checks
we'll bother now to put down to the dis-
and re-appearance of our sort, our nonchalance
subject, for now, to little more than chance.

Your Flowers

I could list your flowers bloomed this spring
and into summer: crocuses,
of course, the snow focuses
its final, crystal meltdown on
for winter's slow, hush denouement.
Last fall's cedar mulch unclings

enough to let your snowdrops hang,
and coalition irises
chase various amaryllises
I can't pretend to tell apart.
I marvel at the whole, op-art
explosive, blooming, big shebang

your colours to my life can bring.
Oh, I might screw up the sequence,
and overlook the consequence
of March's lovely, global warmth
hatching larvae of the moth
that rein your rose camberings in

and rob your heirloom cherry of
its gossamer profusion.
I can't imagine the confusion
you or the forsythia feel
breaking out in early April
when most perennials reserve —

but not because I don't observe
how summer's fragrant alliums
restore our equilibrium
after May's tally of the dead.
I'd order order of bloom restored
but don't go much about such things.

Alighting

High tide, high time,
and through lifting
buildings, people, trees,
into skeins of light
or darkness, whichever
sheds the greater loneness,
scale down to lower ground,
put in, alight from land, and,

still standing, skim first
the coastline's inner harbours,
bringing everything down
to watchful, beneath
the surface the surfaces
of mollusked rocks
or nothing but the gloom
you can speed up on,

the swish you leave behind
surfing whitely out upon itself,
as you reach the outreached
nearly-islands, slow, briefly,
to navigate the spits,

and, if you don't slip up
on an island's high relief
where seafowl squeal and lift,
you come to the open sea's
upheaval of the heavens.

Entrée

Whoso-, where-, and all the other evers
you are or elaborately want:

simply feel along some lines the tremors
of your heart's highstrung desires — all that cant

of entitlement. Hush! O good confessors;
know no end to what you should and can. And can't.

Acknowledgements

Acknowledgement is due to the editors of the following publications where a number of these poems, some in different versions and under different titles, have appeared: *College Green, The Café Review, DoubleTake, Éire-Ireland, Envoi, Fortnight, Free Verse, Green Mountains Review, Harvard Review, Metre, New Hibernia Review, Nua, Poetry Ireland Review, Poetry Review, The Irish Times, The Recorder, The SHOp, The Sunday Tribune* and *TriQuarterly.*

Several poems from this collection have appeared in *Breaking the Skin, Twenty-first Century Irish Writing, Volume Two* (Black Mountain Press, 2002).

'Survival', first published in *The Recorder*, appeared in translation as 'Overleven' by Lut Teck and Griet Vercruysse in *De Brakke Hond.*

I wish to thank Thayer Academy for grants of sabbatical and opportunity which assisted me in this work.

I am grateful for the editorial assistance of Peter Fallon and Bill Tinley.